RACHEL WOJO

Soul
Secure

winning over worry
through God's word

BIBLE READING PLAN & JOURNAL

SOUL SECURE
Bible Reading Plan and Journal
PUBLISHED BY RACHEL WOJO
Copyright © 2017 by Rachel Wojnarowski

Visit **www.rachelwojo.com/shop**

Requests for information should be addressed to rachel@rachelwojo.com

Trade Paperback

ISBN-13: 978-0692894521 (Rachel Wojo LLC)

ISBN-10: 0692894527

Cover design by Rachel Wojnarowski

Photo credit: Bigstock.com

Library of Congress Cataloging-in-Publication Data

Printed in the United States of America
2017—Second Edition--1002

Table of Contents

Table of Contents

A Personal Note from Rachel

Dear Friend,

Thank you for embarking on this journaling experience to a soul free from worry and secure in truth. My goal through Bible reading is to draw closer to Jesus, and I want that for you too!

Through reading daily Bible passages, praying, and listening to God, we're going to nurture and grow our relationship with him. This Bible reading plan and journal is specifically focused on winning over worry through God's Word.

Whether wrestling with fears or reveling in doubts, the temptation to fret over actual or potential issues threatens our security. God is in total control and still on the throne of heaven. When we focus on the truth of his Word, we're reminded that worrying damages everything and accomplishes nothing. This Bible reading plan will help starve worry wasters and instead, feed our thoughts with God's promises.

I.can't.wait!

Rachel

Winning Over Worry with God's Word

Welcome to the Soul Secure Journal. I'm so excited to begin this journey with you! For the next thirty-one days, we are going to dig into God's word and grow closer to Him. Together we'll make the choice to discard thoughts of fear, worry and doubt, replacing them with God's Word by reading and applying it in our daily lives.

> When we are familiar with God's promises, we can expectantly appreciate the future.
> --*One More Step*

Are you ready to gain the victory over worry? You can share what you are learning on social media by using the hashtags #soulsecure #winningoverworry and #biblereadingplan. Or you can just keep it between you and God.

4 Simple Steps
to growing in faith

Step 1:

Pray: Spend some time with God in prayer. Prayer is simply having a conversation with him.

Step 2:

Read the Bible passage for the day one time slowly, soaking in each phrase. Read again if time allows.

Step 3:

Answer the daily question.

Step 4:

Complete the journaling section.

Winning over Worry

In 2 Corinthians 10, Paul writes to the church at Corinth regarding his ministry. He explains a strategy he uses to guard himself from temptations. One small phrase in verse 5 packs a powerful punch.

...take every thought captive to obey Christ.

Throughout this journal, we are going to practice using Paul's strategy against the temptation to worry. By capturing worrisome thoughts before they develop into fear, anxiety, or panic, we will use God's Word to proactively defeat worry before it escalates. You can use the Day 1 example below to help you get started. Happy journaling!

Training Thoughts for a Soul Secure

When I think about:

the future   ,

I start to feel worried. Today's Bible reading passage explains that I do not need to worry because: it does not accomplish anything to work or invest in the future without realizing that God is in control

                                                                  .

I want to replace the worrisome thought mentioned above with the Scripture fact that: I can trust the Lord to provide sweet rest because he loves me   .

Psalm 127:1-5

Day 1

>>>>>>>>>>>>>>>>

Sweet Rest

Pursuing success
on my own will
keep me awake
at night.

Take it to the Lord.
What is one thing I
am worried about
today that I can give
to God right now?

_____
_____
_____
_____
_____
_____
_____
_____

Training Thoughts for a Soul Secure

When I think about

_____,

I start to feel worried. Today's Bible reading passage explains
that I do not need to worry because:

_____
_____
_____.

I want to replace the worrisome thought mentioned above with
the Scripture fact that:

_____
_____.

When I start to feel anxious, I will combat thoughts of worry with one of the following actions:
(Check your focus.)

- o Remind myself that God is in control.
- o Ask the Lord to replace the thought of worry with His truth.
- o Immediately surrender the worrisome thought to the Lord in prayer.
- o Recall the truths I have been journaling.

Pen A Prayer

_____

_____

_____

_____

_____

_____

_____

_____

• • • • • • • • • • • ▶

Strong

Take it to the Lord.
What is one thing I
am worried about
today that I can give
to God right now?

God will calm
my anxious
heart.

_____
_____
_____
_____
_____
_____
_____
_____

Training Thoughts for a Soul Secure

When I think about

_____,

I start to feel worried. Today's Bible reading passage explains
that I do not need to worry because:

_____
_____
_____.

I want to replace the worrisome thought mentioned above with
the Scripture fact that:

_____
_____.

When I start to feel anxious, I will combat thoughts of worry with one of the following actions:
(Check your focus.)

- ○ Remember that God only ever wants the best for me.
- ○ Recognize that God's presence is more powerful than my worries.
- ○ Pray for protection against worry.
- ○ Identify the fear triggering this worry and rebuke it in Jesus' name.

Pen A Prayer

_____

_____

_____

_____

_____

_____

_____

_____

Jeremiah 17:5-10

>>>>>>>>>>>>>>>>>>

Include

Worry is leaving God out of the equation.

Take it to the Lord. What is one thing I am worried about today that I can give to God right now?

_____
_____
_____
_____
_____
_____
_____

Training Thoughts for a Soul Secure

When I think about

_____,

I start to feel worried. Today's Bible reading passage explains that I do not need to worry because:

_____
_____
_____.

I want to replace the worrisome thought mentioned above with the Scripture fact that:

_____
_____.

When I start to feel anxious, I will combat thoughts of worry with one of the following actions:
(Check your focus.)

- o Remind myself that God is in control.
- o Ask the Lord to replace the thought of worry with His truth.
- o Immediately surrender the worrisome thought to the Lord in prayer.
- o Recall the truths I have been journaling.

Pen A Prayer

_____

_____

_____

_____

_____

_____

_____

_____

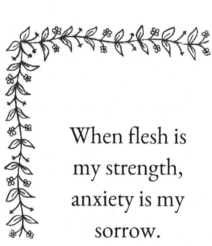

When flesh is
my strength,
anxiety is my
sorrow.

When God is
my strength,
security is my
success.

Matthew 6:22-34

Day 4

• • • • • • • • • • • ▶

Certainty

God is in control
of every minute
of my day.

Take it to the Lord.
What is one thing I
am worried about
today that I can give
to God right now?

_____
_____
_____
_____
_____
_____
_____

Training Thoughts for a Soul Secure

When I think about

_____,

I start to feel worried. Today's Bible reading passage explains
that I do not need to worry because:

_____
_____
_____.

I want to replace the worrisome thought mentioned above with
the Scripture fact that:

_____
_____.

When I start to feel anxious, I will combat thoughts of worry with one of the following actions:
(Check your focus.)

- o Remember that God only ever wants the best for me.
- o Recognize that God's presence is more powerful than my worries.
- o Pray for protection against worry.
- o Identify the fear triggering this worry and rebuke it in Jesus' name.

Pen A Prayer

_____

_____

_____

_____

_____

_____

_____

_____

>>>>>>>>>>>>>>>>>>>

Security

My needs are known
by my Father
before I
ever need them.

Take it to the Lord.
What is one thing I
am worried about
today that I can give
to God right now?

_____
_____
_____
_____
_____
_____
_____

Training Thoughts for a Soul Secure

When I think about

_____,

I start to feel worried. Today's Bible reading passage explains
that I do not need to worry because:

_____
_____
_____.

I want to replace the worrisome thought mentioned above with
the Scripture fact that:

_____
_____.

When I start to feel anxious, I will combat thoughts of worry with one of the following actions:
(Check your focus.)

o Remind myself that God is in control.
o Ask the Lord to replace the thought of worry with His truth.
o Immediately surrender the worrisome thought to the Lord in prayer.
o Recall the truths I have been journaling.

Pen A Prayer

_____

_____

_____

_____

_____

_____

_____

_____

_____

Philippians 4:1-7

Practice

"Do not be anxious"
is a command with
the understood
"you".

Take it to the Lord.
What is one thing I
am worried about
today that I can give
to God right now?

_____
_____
_____
_____
_____
_____
_____

Training Thoughts for a Soul Secure

When I think about

_____,

I start to feel worried. Today's Bible reading passage explains
that I do not need to worry because:

_____
_____
_____.

I want to replace the worrisome thought mentioned above with
the Scripture fact that:

_____
_____.

When I start to feel anxious, I will combat thoughts of worry with one of the following actions:
(Check your focus.)

o Remember that God only ever wants the best for me.
o Recognize that God's presence is more powerful than my worries.
o Pray for protection against worry.
o Identify the fear triggering this worry and rebuke it in Jesus' name.

Pen A Prayer

_____

_____

_____

_____

_____

_____

_____

_____

_____

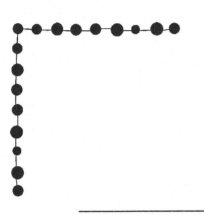

_____,

do

not

be

anxious.

*(Write your name in
the blank.)*

1 Peter 5:1-7

Day 7

>>>>>>>>>>>>>>>>

His Care

When I cast my anxiety on Jesus, my hands are then free to cling to Him.

Take it to the Lord. What is one thing I am worried about today that I can give to God right now?

_____
_____
_____
_____
_____
_____
_____

Training Thoughts for a Soul Secure

When I think about

_____,

I start to feel worried. Today's Bible reading passage explains that I do not need to worry because:

_____
_____
_____.

I want to replace the worrisome thought mentioned above with the Scripture fact that:

_____
_____

When I start to feel anxious, I will combat thoughts of worry with one of the following actions:
(Check your focus.)

o Remind myself that God is in control.
o Ask the Lord to replace the thought of worry with His truth.
o Immediately surrender the worrisome thought to the Lord in prayer.
o Recall the truths I have been journaling.

Pen A Prayer

_____

_____

_____

_____

_____

_____

_____

_____

_____

• • • • • • • • • ►

Decide

There is no need to
be anxious
when God is my
fortress.

Take it to the Lord.
What is one thing I
am worried about
today that I can give
to God right now?

_____
_____
_____
_____
_____
_____
_____

Training Thoughts for a Soul Secure

When I think about

_____,

I start to feel worried. Today's Bible reading passage explains
that I do not need to worry because:

_____
_____
_____.

I want to replace the worrisome thought mentioned above with
the Scripture fact that:

_____
_____.

When I start to feel anxious, I will combat thoughts of worry with one of the following actions:
(Check your focus.)

o   Remember that God only ever wants the best for me.
o   Recognize that God's presence is more powerful than my worries.
o   Pray for protection against worry.
o   Identify the fear triggering this worry and rebuke it in Jesus' name.

Pen A Prayer

_____

_____

_____

_____

_____

_____

_____

_____

_____

Psalm 121:1-8

Help

God protects
and guards me.

Take it to the Lord.
What is one thing I
am worried about
today that I can give
to God right now?

_____
_____
_____
_____
_____
_____
_____

Training Thoughts for a Soul Secure

When I think about

_____,

I start to feel worried. Today's Bible reading passage explains
that I do not need to worry because:

_____
_____
_____.

I want to replace the worrisome thought mentioned above with
the Scripture fact that:

_____
_____.

When I start to feel anxious, I will combat thoughts of worry with one of the following actions:
(Check your focus.)

o Remind myself that God is in control.
o Ask the Lord to replace the thought of worry with His truth.
o Immediately surrender the worrisome thought to the Lord in prayer.
o Recall the truths I have been journaling.

Pen A Prayer

_____

_____

_____

_____

_____

_____

_____

_____

_____

The Lord
keeps watch
over my steps,
he keeps watch over me,
he keeps me from all harm,
and he keeps watch over my life.
I have no reason to worry.
The Lord
is my
Keeper.

Beyond

God will not give me
burdens beyond
what I can bear
because he is my
strength.

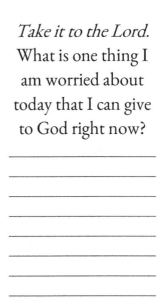

Take it to the Lord.
What is one thing I
am worried about
today that I can give
to God right now?

_____

_____

_____

_____

_____

_____

_____

Training Thoughts for a Soul Secure

When I think about

_____,

I start to feel worried. Today's Bible reading passage explains
that I do not need to worry because:

_____

_____

_____.

I want to replace the worrisome thought mentioned above with
the Scripture fact that:

_____

_____.

When I start to feel anxious, I will combat thoughts of worry with one of the following actions:
(Check your focus.)

- o Remember that God only ever wants the best for me.
- o Recognize that God's presence is more powerful than my worries.
- o Pray for protection against worry.
- o Identify the fear triggering this worry and rebuke it in Jesus' name.

Pen A Prayer

_____

_____

_____

_____

_____

_____

_____

_____

>>>>>>>>>>>>>>>>

Reign

I want Christ's
peace to rule
my heart.

Take it to the Lord.
What is one thing I
am worried about
today that I can give
to God right now?

_____
_____
_____
_____
_____
_____
_____
_____

Training Thoughts for a Soul Secure

When I think about

_____,

I start to feel worried. Today's Bible reading passage explains
that I do not need to worry because:

_____
_____
_____.

I want to replace the worrisome thought mentioned above with
the Scripture fact that:

_____
_____.

When I start to feel anxious, I will combat thoughts of worry with one of the following actions:
(Check your focus.)

o   Remind myself that God is in control.
o   Ask the Lord to replace the thought of worry with His truth.
o   Immediately surrender the worrisome thought to the Lord in prayer.
o   Recall the truths I have been journaling.

Pen A Prayer

_____

_____

_____

_____

_____

_____

_____

_____

Psalm 55:9-19

Day 12

• • • • • • • • • • • • ▶

Relief

Prayer always
brings comfort.

Take it to the Lord.
What is one thing I
am worried about
today that I can give
to God right now?

_____

_____

_____

_____

_____

_____

_____

_____

Training Thoughts for a Soul Secure

When I think about

_____,

I start to feel worried. Today's Bible reading passage explains
that I do not need to worry because:

_____

_____

_____.

I want to replace the worrisome thought mentioned above with
the Scripture fact that:

_____

_____.

When I start to feel anxious, I will combat thoughts of worry with one of the following actions:
(Check your focus.)

o Remember that God only ever wants the best for me.
o Recognize that God's presence is more powerful than my worries.
o Pray for protection against worry.
o Identify the fear triggering this worry and rebuke it in Jesus' name.

Pen A Prayer

_____

_____

_____

_____

_____

_____

_____

_____

Romans 8:28-39

Winner

>>>>>>>>>>>>>>>>

Take it to the Lord.
What is one thing I
am worried about
today that I can give
to God right now?

"If God is for me
who can be
against me?"

_____
_____
_____
_____
_____
_____
_____
_____

Training Thoughts for a Soul Secure

When I think about

_____,

I start to feel worried. Today's Bible reading passage explains
that I do not need to worry because:

_____
_____
_____.

I want to replace the worrisome thought mentioned above with
the Scripture fact that:

_____
_____.

When I start to feel anxious, I will combat thoughts of worry with one of the following actions:
(Check your focus.)

o Remind myself that God is in control.
o Ask the Lord to replace the thought of worry with His truth.
o Immediately surrender the worrisome thought to the Lord in prayer.
o Recall the truths I have been journaling.

Pen A Prayer

_____

_____

_____

_____

_____

_____

_____

_____

I may be
tempted to
worry about:

_____

_____

_____

_____

_____

_____

but NONE
of these things
shall separate
me
from the love
of Jesus Christ.

Day 14

• • • • • • • • • • • • ▶

Protected

Lord, hide me
in the shadow
of your wings.

Take it to the Lord.
What is one thing I
am worried about
today that I can give
to God right now?

_____
_____
_____
_____
_____
_____
_____
_____

Training Thoughts for a Soul Secure

When I think about

_____,

I start to feel worried. Today's Bible reading passage explains
that I do not need to worry because:

_____
_____
_____.

I want to replace the worrisome thought mentioned above with
the Scripture fact that:

_____
_____.

When I start to feel anxious, I will combat thoughts of worry with one of the following actions:
(Check your focus.)

o Remember that God only ever wants the best for me.
o Recognize that God's presence is more powerful than my worries.
o Pray for protection against worry.
o Identify the fear triggering this worry and rebuke it in Jesus' name.

Pen A Prayer

_____

_____

_____

_____

_____

_____

_____

_____

>>>>>>>>>>>>>>>>

Stimulate

I must choose to fan the flame of trusting God and not the flame of worrying.

Take it to the Lord. What is one thing I am worried about today that I can give to God right now?

_____

_____

_____

_____

_____

_____

_____

_____

Training Thoughts for a Soul Secure

When I think about

_____,

I start to feel worried. Today's Bible reading passage explains that I do not need to worry because:

_____

_____

_____.

I want to replace the worrisome thought mentioned above with the Scripture fact that:

_____

_____.

When I start to feel anxious, I will combat thoughts of worry with one of the following actions:
(Check your focus.)

o   Remind myself that God is in control.
o   Ask the Lord to replace the thought of worry with His truth.
o   Immediately surrender the worrisome thought to the Lord in prayer.
o   Recall the truths I have been journaling.

Pen A Prayer

_____

_____

_____

_____

_____

_____

_____

_____

• • • • • • • • • • • ▶

Recognize

God is not only God; he is my God.

Take it to the Lord. What is one thing I am worried about today that I can give to God right now?

_____
_____
_____
_____
_____
_____
_____
_____

Training Thoughts for a Soul Secure

When I think about

_____,

I start to feel worried. Today's Bible reading passage explains that I do not need to worry because:

_____
_____
_____.

I want to replace the worrisome thought mentioned above with the Scripture fact that:

_____
_____.

When I start to feel anxious, I will combat thoughts of worry with one of the following actions:
(Check your focus.)

- o Remember that God only ever wants the best for me.
- o Recognize that God's presence is more powerful than my worries.
- o Pray for protection against worry.
- o Identify the fear triggering this worry and rebuke it in Jesus' name.

Pen A Prayer

_____

_____

_____

_____

_____

_____

_____

_____

A willing servant
learns to trust God
quicker
than a worried saint.

Psalm 91:1-10

>>>>>>>>>>>>>>>>>

Fortress

*Take it to the Lord.
What is one thing I
am worried about
today that I can give
to God right now?*

My God protects
me from all harm.

_____
_____
_____
_____
_____
_____
_____
_____

Training Thoughts for a Soul Secure

When I think about

_____,

I start to feel worried. Today's Bible reading passage explains
that I do not need to worry because:

_____
_____
_____.

I want to replace the worrisome thought mentioned above with
the Scripture fact that:

_____
_____.

When I start to feel anxious, I will combat thoughts of worry with one of the following actions:
(Check your focus.)

○ Remind myself that God is in control.
○ Ask the Lord to replace the thought of worry with His truth.
○ Immediately surrender the worrisome thought to the Lord in prayer.
○ Recall the truths I have been journaling.

Pen A Prayer

_____

_____

_____

_____

_____

_____

_____

_____

Reinforcement

I can ask the Lord
to send angels to
protect me from
worry at any time.

· · · · · · · · · · · · ▶

Take it to the Lord.
What is one thing I
am worried about
today that I can give
to God right now?

_____
_____
_____
_____
_____
_____
_____
_____

Training Thoughts for a Soul Secure

When I think about

_____,

I start to feel worried. Today's Bible reading passage explains
that I do not need to worry because:

_____
_____
_____.

I want to replace the worrisome thought mentioned above with
the Scripture fact that:

_____
_____.

When I start to feel anxious, I will combat thoughts of
worry with one of the following actions:
(Check your focus.)

- o Remember that God only ever wants the best for
  me.
- o Recognize that God's presence is more powerful
  than my worries.
- o Pray for protection against worry.
- o Identify the fear triggering this worry and rebuke it
  in Jesus' name.

Pen A Prayer

_____

_____

_____

_____

_____

_____

_____

_____

Psalm 112:1-10

Day 19

>>>>>>>>>>>>>>>>>>

Delight

Take it to the Lord.
What is one thing I
am worried about
today that I can give
to God right now?

It is well
with my soul.

_____
_____
_____
_____
_____
_____
_____
_____

Training Thoughts for a Soul Secure

When I think about

_____,

I start to feel worried. Today's Bible reading passage explains
that I do not need to worry because:

_____
_____
_____.

I want to replace the worrisome thought mentioned above with
the Scripture fact that:

_____
_____.

When I start to feel anxious, I will combat thoughts of worry with one of the following actions:
(Check your focus.)

○ Remind myself that God is in control.
○ Ask the Lord to replace the thought of worry with His truth.
○ Immediately surrender the worrisome thought to the Lord in prayer.
○ Recall the truths I have been journaling.

Pen A Prayer

_____

_____

_____

_____

_____

_____

_____

_____

Psalm 56:1-13

Day 20

. . . . ▶

Relationship

While worry and
fear are BFF's
God is my BFF.

Take it to the Lord.
What is one thing I
am worried about
today that I can give
to God right now?

_____
_____
_____
_____
_____
_____
_____
_____

Training Thoughts for a Soul Secure

When I think about

_____,

I start to feel worried. Today's Bible reading passage explains
that I do not need to worry because:

_____
_____
_____.

I want to replace the worrisome thought mentioned above with
the Scripture fact that:

_____
_____.

When I start to feel anxious, I will combat thoughts of worry with one of the following actions:
(Check your focus.)

- o Remember that God only ever wants the best for me.
- o Recognize that God's presence is more powerful than my worries.
- o Pray for protection against worry.
- o Identify the fear triggering this worry and rebuke it in Jesus' name.

Pen A Prayer

_____

_____

_____

_____

_____

_____

_____

_____

Galatians 6:1-10

Day 21

>>>>>>>>>>>>>>>>>>

Choice

I can dwell on the worrisome details or I can focus on what the Spirit speaks.

Take it to the Lord. What is one thing I am worried about today that I can give to God right now?

_____

_____

_____

_____

_____

_____

_____

Training Thoughts for a Soul Secure

When I think about

_____,

I start to feel worried. Today's Bible reading passage explains that I do not need to worry because:

_____

_____

_____.

I want to replace the worrisome thought mentioned above with the Scripture fact that:

_____

_____.

When I start to feel anxious, I will combat thoughts of worry with one of the following actions:
(Check your focus.)

- ○ Remind myself that God is in control.
- ○ Ask the Lord to replace the thought of worry with His truth.
- ○ Immediately surrender the worrisome thought to the Lord in prayer.
- ○ Recall the truths I have been journaling.

Pen A Prayer

_____

_____

_____

_____

_____

_____

_____

_____

•••••••••••▶

Worry
does not
empty tomorrow
of its sorrow;
it empties today
of its strength.

Corrie Ten Boom

◀••••••••••••

Steadfast

Trade anxiety for
the Anchor.

• • • • • • • • • • • ▶

Take it to the Lord.
What is one thing I
am worried about
today that I can give
to God right now?

_____
_____
_____
_____
_____
_____
_____
_____

Training Thoughts for a Soul Secure

When I think about

_____,

I start to feel worried. Today's Bible reading passage explains
that I do not need to worry because:

_____
_____
_____.

I want to replace the worrisome thought mentioned above with
the Scripture fact that:

_____
_____.

When I start to feel anxious, I will combat thoughts of worry with one of the following actions:
(Check your focus.)

o   Remember that God only ever wants the best for me.
o   Recognize that God's presence is more powerful than my worries.
o   Pray for protection against worry.
o   Identify the fear triggering this worry and rebuke it in Jesus' name.

Pen A Prayer

_____

_____

_____

_____

_____

_____

_____

_____

>>>>>>>>>>>>>>>>>>

Determine

Choosing not to
worry is the
choice that leads
to peace.

Take it to the Lord.
What is one thing I
am worried about
today that I can give
to God right now?

_____

_____

_____

_____

_____

_____

Training Thoughts for a Soul Secure

When I think about

_____,

I start to feel worried. Today's Bible reading passage explains
that I do not need to worry because:

_____

_____

_____.

I want to replace the worrisome thought mentioned above with
the Scripture fact that:

_____

_____.

When I start to feel anxious, I will combat thoughts of worry with one of the following actions:
(Check your focus.)

o Remind myself that God is in control.
o Ask the Lord to replace the thought of worry with His truth.
o Immediately surrender the worrisome thought to the Lord in prayer.
o Recall the truths I have been journaling.

Pen A Prayer

_____

_____

_____

_____

_____

_____

_____

_____

Why worry, when you can pray?
Trust Jesus, He will make a way.
Don't be like doubtful Thomas,
Just rest upon His promise,
Why worry, worry, worry,
when you can pray?

Hymn, Why Worry When You Can Pray?
Alfred B. Smith,
John Peterson

Psalm 73:21-28

• • • • • • • • • • • • ▶

Purposeful

God is the
strength of my
portion forever.

Take it to the Lord.
What is one thing I
am worried about
today that I can give
to God right now?

_____
_____
_____
_____
_____
_____
_____
_____

Training Thoughts for a Soul Secure

When I think about

_____,

I start to feel worried. Today's Bible reading passage explains
that I do not need to worry because:

_____
_____
_____.

I want to replace the worrisome thought mentioned above with
the Scripture fact that:

_____
_____.

When I start to feel anxious, I will combat thoughts of worry with one of the following actions:
(Check your focus.)

- o Remember that God only ever wants the best for me.
- o Recognize that God's presence is more powerful than my worries.
- o Pray for protection against worry.
- o Identify the fear triggering this worry and rebuke it in Jesus' name.

Pen A Prayer

_____

_____

_____

_____

_____

_____

_____

_____

Psalm 18:1-13

Exchange

When I praise God
who is worthy, I
realize the futility
of worry.

>>>>>>>>>>>>>>>>>

Take it to the Lord.
What is one thing I
am worried about
today that I can give
to God right now?

_____
_____
_____
_____
_____
_____
_____

Training Thoughts for a Soul Secure

When I think about

_____,

I start to feel worried. Today's Bible reading passage explains
that I do not need to worry because:

_____
_____
_____.

I want to replace the worrisome thought mentioned above with
the Scripture fact that:

_____
_____.

When I start to feel anxious, I will combat thoughts of worry with one of the following actions:
(Check your focus.)

o   Remind myself that God is in control.
o   Ask the Lord to replace the thought of worry with His truth.
o   Immediately surrender the worrisome thought to the Lord in prayer.
o   Recall the truths I have been journaling.

Pen A Prayer

_____

_____

_____

_____

_____

_____

_____

_____

_____

I want prayer to be
my first response,
not my last resort.

Rachel Wojo, One More Step

Psalm 18:14-29

· · · · · · · · · · · · ▶

Affirmation

I want to trade
thoughts of
confrontation for
the fact that the
Lord is my
support.

Take it to the Lord.
What is one thing I
am worried about
today that I can give
to God right now?

_____
_____
_____
_____
_____
_____
_____
_____

Training Thoughts for a Soul Secure

When I think about

_____,

I start to feel worried. Today's Bible reading passage explains
that I do not need to worry because:

_____
_____
_____.

I want to replace the worrisome thought mentioned above with
the Scripture fact that:

_____
_____.

When I start to feel anxious, I will combat thoughts of
worry with one of the following actions:
(Check your focus.)

o Remember that God only ever wants the best for
  me.
o Recognize that God's presence is more powerful
  than my worries.
o Pray for protection against worry.
o Identify the fear triggering this worry and rebuke it
  in Jesus' name.

Pen A Prayer

_____

_____

_____

_____

_____

_____

_____

_____

Stable

Instead of worrying
where God's path
is leading, I want to
focus on where His
light is shining.

Take it to the Lord.
What is one thing I
am worried about
today that I can give
to God right now?

_____
_____
_____
_____
_____
_____
_____

Training Thoughts for a Soul Secure

When I think about

_____,

I start to feel worried. Today's Bible reading passage explains
that I do not need to worry because:

_____
_____
_____.

I want to replace the worrisome thought mentioned above with
the Scripture fact that:

_____
_____

When I start to feel anxious, I will combat thoughts of worry with one of the following actions:
(Check your focus.)

- o Remind myself that God is in control.
- o Ask the Lord to replace the thought of worry with His truth.
- o Immediately surrender the worrisome thought to the Lord in prayer.
- o Recall the truths I have been journaling.

Pen A Prayer

_____

_____

_____

_____

_____

_____

_____

_____

Psalm 18:40-50 **Day 28**

Unshakeable

God does not
change when the
world is turned
upside down.

• • • • • • • • • • • • ▶

Take it to the Lord.
What is one thing I
am worried about
today that I can give
to God right now?

_____
_____
_____
_____
_____
_____
_____

Training Thoughts for a Soul Secure

When I think about

_____,

I start to feel worried. Today's Bible reading passage explains
that I do not need to worry because:

_____
_____
_____.

I want to replace the worrisome thought mentioned above with
the Scripture fact that:

_____
_____.

When I start to feel anxious, I will combat thoughts of worry with one of the following actions:
(Check your focus.)

o Remember that God only ever wants the best for me.
o Recognize that God's presence is more powerful than my worries.
o Pray for protection against worry.
o Identify the fear triggering this worry and rebuke it in Jesus' name.

Pen A Prayer

_____

_____

_____

_____

_____

_____

_____

_____

>>>>>>>>>>>>>>>>

Knowledge

My path is filled
with worry and
doubt; His path
overflows with
peace and
confidence

*Take it to the Lord.
What is one thing I
am worried about
today that I can give
to God right now?*

_____
_____
_____
_____
_____
_____
_____

Training Thoughts for a Soul Secure

When I think about

_____,

I start to feel worried. Today's Bible reading passage explains
that I do not need to worry because:

_____
_____
_____.

I want to replace the worrisome thought mentioned above with
the Scripture fact that:

_____
_____.

When I start to feel anxious, I will combat thoughts of worry with one of the following actions:
(Check your focus.)

o Remind myself that God is in control.
o Ask the Lord to replace the thought of worry with His truth.
o Immediately surrender the worrisome thought to the Lord in prayer.
o Recall the truths I have been journaling.

Pen A Prayer

_____

_____

_____

_____

_____

_____

_____

_____

Psalm 25:11-22

Day 30

● ● ● ● ● ● ● ● ● ● ● ● ▶

Patience

Waiting on God's timing is the best life preservation method.

Take it to the Lord. What is one thing I am worried about today that I can give to God right now?

_____
_____
_____
_____
_____
_____

Training Thoughts for a Soul Secure

When I think about

_____,

I start to feel worried. Today's Bible reading passage explains that I do not need to worry because:

_____
_____
_____.

I want to replace the worrisome thought mentioned above with the Scripture fact that:

_____
_____.

When I start to feel anxious, I will combat thoughts of worry with one of the following actions:
(Check your focus.)

o Remember that God only ever wants the best for me.
o Recognize that God's presence is more powerful than my worries.
o Pray for protection against worry.
o Identify the fear triggering this worry and rebuke it in Jesus' name.

Pen A Prayer

_____

_____

_____

_____

_____

_____

_____

_____

_____

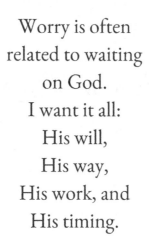

Worry is often
related to waiting
on God.
I want it all:
His will,
His way,
His work, and
His timing.

Psalm 19:1-14

Hidden

Often no one but God and I know that I am in a worry mode.

>>>>>>>>>>>>>>>>>

Take it to the Lord.
What is one thing I am worried about today that I can give to God right now?

_____
_____
_____
_____
_____
_____
_____
_____

Training Thoughts for a Soul Secure

When I think about

_____,

I start to feel worried. Today's Bible reading passage explains that I do not need to worry because:

_____
_____
_____.

I want to replace the worrisome thought mentioned above with the Scripture fact that:

_____
_____.

When I start to feel anxious, I will combat thoughts of worry with one of the following actions:
(Check your focus.)

- o Remind myself that God is in control.
- o Ask the Lord to replace the thought of worry with His truth.
- o Immediately surrender the worrisome thought to the Lord in prayer.
- o Recall the truths I have been journaling.

Pen A Prayer

_____

_____

_____

_____

_____

_____

_____

_____

Put a Bow on It!

You did it! You read your Bible for 31 days in a row!

Throughout this month of Scripture reading, I've been reminded that while worry tempts, faith trusts. Replacing upsetting thoughts with reminders of God's truth curbs worry before it can heighten.

I pray that as you've walked this 31-day path, you've practiced training your thoughts in obedience to Christ and you've enjoyed winning over worry through God's Word.

May you continue to rest in God's promises as a soul secure in the Anchor of hope!

Thanks for joining me on this journey through the Bible. Discover more Bible reading plans & journals at rachelwojo.com/shop.

Additional Notes

About the Author

Rachel "Wojo" Wojnarowski is wife to Matt and mom to seven wonderful kids. Her greatest passion is inspiring others to welcome Jesus into their lives and enjoy the abundant life he offers.

As a sought-after blogger and writer, she sees thousands of readers visit her blog daily. Rachel leads community ladies' Bible studies in central Ohio and serves as an event planner and speaker. In her "free time" she crochets, knits, and sews handmade clothing. Okay, not really. She enjoys running and she's a tech geek at heart.

Reader, writer, speaker, and dreamer, Rachel can be found on her website at **www.RachelWojo.com**.

Free Bible Study Video Series

If you enjoyed this Bible reading plan & journal, then you'll love Rachel's free video Bible study to help you find strength for difficult seasons of life! **http://rachelwojo.com/free-bible-study-video-series-for-one-more-step/**

Feel like giving up?

Are you ready to quit? Give up? But deep down, you want to figure out how to keep on keeping on?

Like you, Rachel has faced experiences that crushed her dreams of the perfect life: a failed marriage, a daughter's heartbreaking diagnosis, and more. In this book, she transparently shares her pain and empathizes with yours, then points you to the path of God's Word, where you'll find hope to carry you forward. One More Step gives you permission to ache freely—and helps you believe that life won't always be this hard. No matter the circumstances you face, through these pages you'll learn to...

- persevere through out-of-control circumstances and gain a more intimate relationship with Jesus
- run to God's Word when discouragement strikes
- replace feelings of despair with truths of Scripture

If you enjoyed this Bible reading plan and journal, then you'll love:

http://rachelwojo.com/shop

Made in the USA
Columbia, SC
01 July 2020